WEDDING PLANNER PROJECT

Thank you for everything that you don't even know you did. Love you

WEDDING PLANNER PROJECT

Chell Little

a workbook

TATE PUBLISHING & *Enterprises*

Wedding Planner Project
Copyright © 2010 by Chell Little. All rights reserved.

No part of this publication may be reproduced, stored in a retrieval system or transmitted in any way by any means, electronic, mechanical, photocopy, recording or otherwise without the prior permission of the author except as provided by USA copyright law.

This book is designed to provide accurate and authoritative information with regard to the subject matter covered. This information is given with the understanding that neither the author nor Tate Publishing, LLC is engaged in rendering legal, professional advice. Since the details of your situation are fact dependent, you should additionally seek the services of a competent professional.

The opinions expressed by the author are not necessarily those of Tate Publishing, LLC.

Published by Tate Publishing & Enterprises, LLC
127 E. Trade Center Terrace | Mustang, Oklahoma 73064 USA
1.888.361.9473 | www.tatepublishing.com

Tate Publishing is committed to excellence in the publishing industry. The company reflects the philosophy established by the founders, based on Psalm 68:11,
"The Lord gave the word and great was the company of those who published it."

Book design copyright © 2010 by Tate Publishing, LLC. All rights reserved.
Cover design by Amber Gulilat
Interior design by Jeff Fisher

Published in the United States of America

ISBN: 978-1-61663-972-3
1. Reference, Weddings
2. Reference, Personal & Practical Guides
10.08.23

TABLE OF CONTENTS

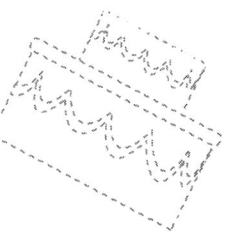

Table of Contents 5
Introduction 7
What This Is 9
Things to Think About 11
The Foundation 17
Budget 19
To Do 21
Rings 23
The Wedding Party 27
Wedding Party Gifts 31
Ceremony 33
Officiate 37
Guest List 39
Invitations, Announcements, Thank-you Notes,
    and Programs 45
Your Vows 49
The Dresses 51

Beauty (Hair and Nails) 55

The Suits 57

Florist 59

Flowers 61

Caterers 65

The Food 67

The Cake 69

Reception 71

Reception Décor 75

Seating Arrangements 77

Favors 83

Pictures / Video 85

Music 87

The Dances 89

Gift List 91

Transportation 95

The Honeymoon 97

The Rehearsal Dinner 99

The Way It Goes 101

Delegate 103

Finishing Touches 107

Conclusion 113

INTRODUCTION

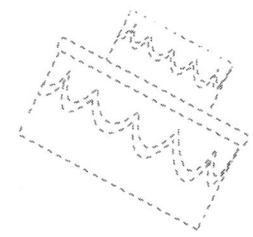

This book will help you in planning your wedding. How do I know? Because not only am I a bride (or was a few years ago), but I have also helped others plan and organize their weddings. At one time in my life I was a florist. I have put flowers together for many a wedding and many a fussy bride. I have had to special order flowers at the last minute; I have had to change designs at the last minute. This part has taught me that brides are a sensitive creature and that weddings have to be perfect.

At another time in my life I was a caterer. We worked on setting up the wedding and the reception. We handled the food, and *every* detail had to be perfect. If one single flower was out of place, it was our job to make it right.

I have helped a lot of friends and family members plan their weddings. I started off by watching my mom plan my sister's wedding. That is were I got my first look at the price and planning of a wedding. Then I used a lot of the things that I learned from my mom to help friends plan their weddings. (Not to mention watching a lot of people through being a florist and a caterer.)

Then there was my wedding. I planned my wedding and only paid $1,500. I know that isn't the norm, and that is okay. But it does prove that if you are on a budget it can be done. The wedding was beautiful, and it fit my husband and me perfectly. When I planned my wedding, I used a lot of the advice that I give in this book.

So remember, if your wedding is to be a million-dollar event or a $1,500 event, it can be beautiful, perfect, and everything you want it to be. Congrats on your engagement. Now let's get started on planning the main event!

WHAT THIS IS

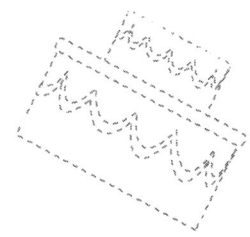

When your wedding day comes around, the organization of the event isn't always easy, and hiring a wedding planner is not always affordable. With all of the other expenses that can pop up at a moment's notice, wouldn't it be nice to know that you have options? Organization can do that for you. In this book you will find the sections for you to organize your wedding plans down to the last detail. I have provided tips for organization, as well as helpful ways to make your big day beautiful and a lot less stressful. In these pages you will find templates to fill out for finding your dream dress, information and pricing on your florist, and even the dreams and pricing for your perfect honeymoon. You can do this by yourself; all you need is a little organization.

This book can be set up in whatever way is easiest for you. There are pages for pictures and templates for you to fill out. Feel free to make copies of the templates as you need them. I hope that the templates and the information on some of the tip pages are helpful to you. This is a tool to help you do it yourself and keep you organized in the process. Just remember when you are doing anything involving the wedding to keep this with you.

I have left some of the sections blank. That is part of the customization built in for you. If you feel that I have forgotten something that is necessary to the planning of a wedding, please feel free to e-mail me and let me know. I am always looking for ways to improve upon my products. If you have any questions, comments, or ideas, please let me know.

Please visit my website at *http://www.chell-little.com*

Thank you and enjoy!

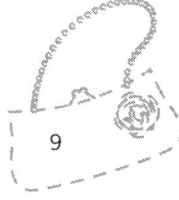

THINGS TO THINK ABOUT

Remember in planning a wedding and in using this book that you don't have to do it all. If you are doing a simple wedding, then go simple. If you are doing huge, then go huge. It is all about you. This book has the ability to be customized for you! Use what you want and forget the rest. Everything in this book is to help you make the best wedding for you.

Remember to keep your receipts from everything. If you realize that you don't like something or something goes wrong, you have a receipt. This is an important fact with any major purchase, and this is a major event. Get a receipt for your deposits and for the final payoff amount. If you are making payments on something, get a receipt for every payment. Sometimes with big companies, things fall through the cracks. It even happens with small companies. Get a receipt, keep it, and use it if you have to. This is your big day; don't let anything mess it up.

Remember to get everything in writing, especially pick-up or delivery dates and times. If the company is going to deliver an item for you wedding, have them put it in writing. If you can get the name of the person who is going to deliver it and the time, do so. Make sure that you write out exactly where the person is to deliver the item. If you write it down or type it up for them, there should be no mistake. Also, call the day before the delivery to make sure that they have not lost any information. You can also assign someone who is not in the wedding party to be your delivery coordinator. This person will know where all of the deliveries are to go and whom he or she is meeting with. If you choose to do this, make sure the delivery person knows the name of your coordinator. Your coordinator can also be your pick-up person. If a company will not deliver an item, the coordinator can pick it up for you.

Remember to do your research. This is important. Before you just buy something because you think it is what you want or hire someone because you're in a hurry, make sure! Go online and look around. Go to wedding expos. Go to dress shops. Do the legwork. You will be surprised what you find—the good, the bad, and the perfect! You will find everything you are looking for and more.

Remember when you are looking at flowers that it is easier to get flowers that are in season. Yes, you want what you want. But they will be easier to find, less expensive, and fresher if you pick flowers that are in season.

Remember to write everything down. For example, if you are getting your dream dress altered in any way, write down what the seamstress says is going to happen. If she is going to move the zipper, write it down. If she is going to take it in an inch, write it down. These things are important. That way when things change, you know exactly what was supposed to happen and the changes that were made. You can use a simple folder or binder and stick it inside the front or back cover of the book. That way, all your receipts, contracts, research, and everything else, is all in one neatly organized place.

Remember to get a camera and use it. We all know that you will not be going dress shopping by yourself. So have whoever is going with you take pictures. That makes it easy to remember exactly what you liked, loved, and hated about each dress. If you're cake shopping, take pictures of samples. Write down your thoughts on taste and put them and the pictures together so that you remember what you liked and what you didn't. You can do this with everything for the wedding, from the dress to the flowers to the cake. Remember that when it comes to food, ask to taste it! Cake, meat, salad, pasta, desserts, everything! If you don't like the way it tastes, why would you have it at your wedding? Make sure that your soon-to-be also tastes everything. You and he are the only ones that have to be pleased. Don't like it, don't get it!

Remember when writing the guest list that not everyone is going to show. If they do, you're lucky. Also remember that sometimes you have to limit the amount of people you invite due to

your budget. That's okay too. The most important people should be invited. If that is everybody you know, so be it. But really think about it before you jump in with both feet.

Remember to be creative, be expressive, and be you! This is about you and your soon-to-be hubby. If you guys want to get married wearing all black and stand on your heads during the ceremony, do it! Don't let anybody influence what you want. This is not their day; it's yours! If you can't get exactly what you want, make it. If you can't afford everything on your dream list, make it. Make sure that you include friends and family to make it fun.

Remember that you have options. There are pages in this book that will help make your choices easier. Remember when you are shopping around for something to write down where you found what you are looking for and then see if you can find it somewhere else. Why? Because you might be able to find it better, cheaper, or even exactly what you want and not have to compromise.

Remember that if you can cut some of your budget in areas that aren't all that important to you, you can spend more in areas that are important to you. Keep to your budget the best that you can. That just makes it easier for everybody involved, especially if you're paying for the wedding yourself or your parents are. You would like them to be able to retire one day, right?

Remember when planning a wedding and working on a budget that you have options. If you are paying for this yourself and don't have that great a budget, talk to the parents. Traditionally, the parents of the bride would pay for the wedding and the parents of the groom would pay for the rehearsal dinner. But nowadays that isn't always the case. You can ask the parents of either side, or both, to make a contribution to your wedding fund. Most parents have no problem helping out, but that doesn't make the conversation any easier. So sit down to a nice dinner and just be honest. You could ask that they pitch in by giving you money or ask them to help by buying certain elements for the wedding.

Remember that the off times, off times meaning fall and winter, for a wedding are going to cost you less. If you have all the money to pay for everything you want the way you want it, go for it. But if you are on a budget, remember the off times. Sundays are always busy days for weddings. The days that are less busy are Fridays and Saturdays. Not to mention, the off-season months. If you are trying to book a wedding from May to September, you better be doing it a year in advance. You are not the only one who thinks a spring or summer wedding would be great. But if you are saving money, shoot for November through April. They are less busy for weddings, and you will save money in the process. Saving money in the off season is not just for the wedding. Think of your honeymoon too. Flying on off days is cheaper. Keep that in mind to save money also.

Remember that you can send the invitations as early as two months or as late as three weeks before the wedding. Remember that the busy seasons are also vacation seasons for some. This gives people time to ask for time off and is normally enough time so that they don't make plans for the date of your wedding. But the earlier you send them, the more time you have to fill seats if some can't attend.

Remember to register. Then remember to put a note in the wedding invitations telling guests where you are registered. This will eliminate the possibility of you getting ten toasters. This also makes it easy for people to get you what you need to start your life together. When you register, don't just go to the expensive stores. Not everybody will be able to afford that sterling silver tea set you were looking at. So find three really good stores, one that is a little on the expensive side, one in the middle, and one that is more affordable. That way you get what you want, everybody can afford a gift, and you don't end up with the same thing from everybody.

Remember to send thank-you notes. This is important. You don't have to send them as you are leaving the reception, but they should be sent in a timely manner. There are pages in this book that make is easy to remember who gave/sent you what. When you are opening the gifts, have your maid of honor write the names of who gave you the gift and what it was. That way you will be able to do the thank-you cards with ease.

Remember that the pages in this book can be copied. If you run out of space or if you have more options to think about than there are pages, make copies. Don't limit yourself to what is in here; make more. From the pages to the empty sections, use the space up and make copies if you have to. That is the beauty of this book. You can make it yours!

Most of all remember, if you ever wanted a time to be the center of attention…this is it! And it is all about you! Enjoy!

THE FOUNDATION

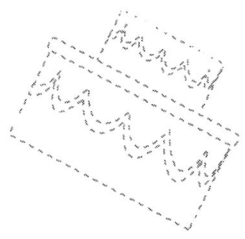

This is all of the final information, the details. Write it out. Then you have all of the information in one place. Remember, you are not the only person who will need to find information in this book.

Wedding Date: _____

Time: _____

Colors: _____

Theme: _____

Number of Bridesmaids: _____

Number of Groomsmen: _____

Place of Ceremony: _____

_____

Place of Reception: _____

_____

Florist: _____

Entertainment: _____

Photographer: _____

Caterer: _____

Cake: _____

Officiate: _____

Invites (where): _____

Favors (where): _____

Dress (where): _____

Tux (where): _____

Transportation: _____

BUDGET

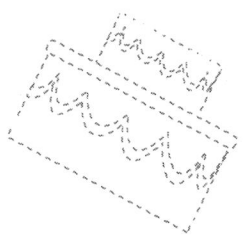

Remember, you can do amazing things on a small budget. Use your budget wisely. This section is so that you can stay on track. Remembering what your budget is and what you are paying as you go is just part of budgeting.

*Amount you are able to spend total:*_____

The Breakdown

Venue:_____

Reception:_____

Dress:_____

Tux:_____

Cake:_____

Catering:_____

Music:_____

Transportation:_____

Décor:_____

Flowers:_____

Rings:_____

Beauty:_____

Invitations:_____

Thank-you Notes:_____

Announcements:_____

Programs:_____

Bridal Underclothes:_____

Groom Extra:_____

Favors:_____

Photographs:_____

Video:_____

Honeymoon:_____

Officiate:_____

Wedding party gifts:_____

Total Spent: _____ *Over Budget:* _____

TO DO

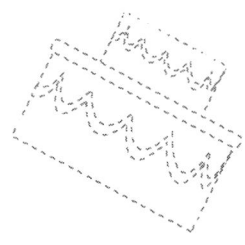

Write out what needs to be done. You can make copies of this section to hand out to people that you have delegated to or just to remind yourself of the final steps before the steps down the aisle.

Date:_____

Task:_____

_____

_____

_____

Date Completed:_____

Date:_____

Task:_____

_____

_____

_____

Date Completed:_____

Date:_____

Task:_____

_____

_____

_____

Date Completed:_____

Date:_____

Task:_____

_____

_____

_____

Date Completed:_____

Date:_____

Task:_____

_____

_____

_____

Date Completed:_____

RINGS

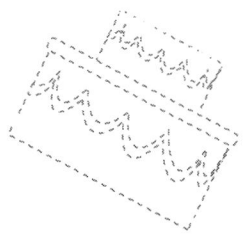

This is a trip that you and your soon-to-be hubby take alone. These are the symbols of love that you will wear forever. Make them special. Call around and see if someone can make your rings for you, or shop around to find just what you're looking for.

Name:_____   Description:_____
Phone Number:_____   _____
Address:_____   _____
_____
_____   Thoughts/feelings:_____
Price:_____   _____
Deposit:_____   _____

Front View   *Stone/Setting Detail*

Name:_____ Description:_____
Phone Number:_____ _____
Address:_____ _____
_____
_____   Thoughts/feelings:_____
Price:_____ _____
Deposit:_____ _____

Front View   *Stone/Setting Detail*

Name:_____ Description:_____
Phone Number:_____ _____
Address:_____ _____
_____
_____ Thoughts/feelings:_____
Price:_____ _____
Deposit:_____ _____

Front View *Stone/Setting Detail*

Name:_____ Description:_____

Phone Number:_____ _____

Address:_____ _____

_____

_____ Thoughts/feelings:_____

Price:_____ _____

Deposit:_____ _____

Front View *Stone/Setting Detail*

THE WEDDING PARTY

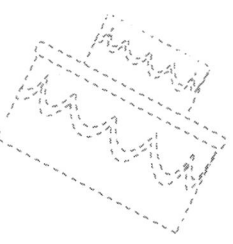

Remember that you are not the only person who will be referencing this book. If your mother, sister, father, soon-to-be hubby, etc. need to get a hold of someone in the party, they should not have to look far for all of the information.

Maid of Honor

Home Number:_____
Cell Number:_____
Dress Size:_____
Shoe Size:_____

Best Man

Home Number:_____
Cell Number:_____
Shirt Size:_____
Coat Size:_____
Pant Size:_____
Shoe Size:_____

Bridesmaids

Name:_____ Name:_____
Home Number:_____ Home Number:_____
Cell Number:_____ Cell Number:_____
Dress Size:_____ Dress Size:_____
Shoe Size:_____ Shoe Size:_____

Name:_____ Name:_____
Home Number:_____ Home Number:_____
Cell Number:_____ Cell Number:_____
Dress Size:_____ Dress Size:_____
Shoe Size:_____ Shoe Size:_____

Name:_____ Name:_____
Home Number:_____ Home Number:_____
Cell Number:_____ Cell Number:_____
Dress Size:_____ Dress Size:_____
Shoe Size:_____ Shoe Size:_____

Groomsman:

Name:_____
Home Number:_____
Cell Number:_____
Shirt Size:_____
Coat Size:_____
Pant Size:_____
Shoe Size:_____

Name:_____
Home Number:_____
Cell Number:_____
Shirt Size:_____
Coat Size:_____
Pant Size:_____
Shoe Size:_____

Name:_____
Home Number:_____
Cell Number:_____
Shirt Size:_____
Coat Size:_____
Pant Size:_____
Shoe Size:_____

Name:_____
Home Number:_____
Cell Number:_____
Shirt Size:_____
Coat Size:_____
Pant Size:_____
Shoe Size:_____

Name:_____
Home Number:_____
Cell Number:_____
Shirt Size:_____
Coat Size:_____
Pant Size:_____
Shoe Size:_____

Name:_____
Home Number:_____
Cell Number:_____
Shirt Size:_____
Coat Size:_____
Pant Size:_____
Shoe Size:_____

WEDDING PARTY GIFTS

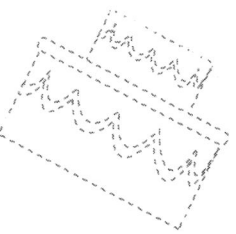

Remember the bridal party. They have been chosen to stand by you when you get married, and there should be a special thank you for doing so. Pick a few little things for your bridal party to say how you feel.

Maid of Honor: _____
_____

Bridesmaids: _____
_____

Best Man: _____
_____

Groomsmen: _____
_____

Ring Bearer: _____
_____

Flower Girl: _____
_____

CEREMONY

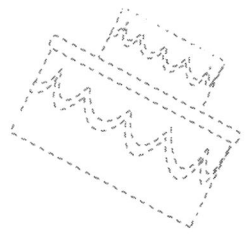

This section is to help you find the perfect place to have your ceremony. You have the space to price compare, space compare, and find what is best for you.

Name:_____

Phone Number:_____

Address:_____

_____

_____

Dates Available:_____

_____

Times Available:_____

_____

Price:_____

What is provided for the price:_____

_____

_____

Thoughts/feelings:_____

_____

_____

Name:_____
Phone Number:_____
Address:_____
_____
_____
Dates Available:_____
_____
Times Available:_____
_____
Price:_____
What is provided for the price:_____
_____
_____
Thoughts/feelings:_____
_____
_____

Name:_____

Phone Number:_____

Address:_____

_____

_____

Dates Available:_____

_____

Times Available:_____

_____

Price:_____

What is provided for the price:_____

_____

_____

Thoughts/feelings:_____

_____

_____

OFFICIATE

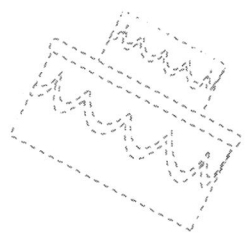

Now, if you have a family member, friend, or religious figure that will be doing the ceremony for you, great! That leaves this section pretty much blank for you. However, if you don't know someone who will be doing the ceremony for you, then use this section to the fullest.

There are several kinds of officiates that you can use. You can take the religious route, which is pretty traditional. You can have a nondenominational officiate, be it that you aren't religious or that you are both are of different religions and this is just easier. Or if you are feeling really adventurous, you could have Elvis. Either way, you need to talk to different people and see what works best for you.

Name:_____

Phone Number:_____

Address:_____

_____

_____

Cost:_____

Deposit:_____

Thoughts/Feelings:_____

_____

_____

Name:_____

Phone Number:_____

Address:_____

_____

_____

Cost:_____

Deposit:_____

Thoughts/Feelings:_____

_____

_____

Name:_____

Phone Number:_____

Address:_____

_____

_____

Cost:_____

Deposit:_____

Thoughts/Feelings:_____

_____

_____

GUEST LIST

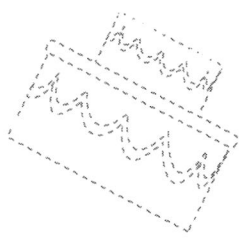

Bride's:

1. _____
2. _____
3. _____
4. _____
5. _____
6. _____
7. _____
8. _____
9. _____
10. _____
11. _____
12. _____
13. _____
14. _____

Groom's:

1. _____
2. _____
3. _____
4. _____
5. _____
6. _____
7. _____
8. _____
9. _____
10. _____
11. _____
12. _____
13. _____
14. _____

Bride's:

15. _____
16. _____
17. _____
18. _____
19. _____
20. _____
21. _____
22. _____
23. _____
24. _____
25. _____
26. _____
27. _____
28. _____
29. _____
30. _____
31. _____
32. _____
33. _____

Groom's:

15. _____
16. _____
17. _____
18. _____
19. _____
20. _____
21. _____
22. _____
23. _____
24. _____
25. _____
26. _____
27. _____
28. _____
29. _____
30. _____
31. _____
32. _____
33. _____

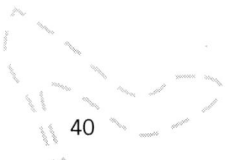

Bride's:

34. _____
35. _____
36. _____
37. _____
38. _____
39. _____
40. _____
41. _____
42. _____
43. _____
44. _____
45. _____
46. _____
47. _____
48. _____
49. _____
50. _____
51. _____
52. _____

Groom's:

34. _____
35. _____
36. _____
37. _____
38. _____
39. _____
40. _____
41. _____
42. _____
43. _____
44. _____
45. _____
46. _____
47. _____
48. _____
49. _____
50. _____
51. _____
52. _____

Bride's:

53. _____
54. _____
55. _____
56. _____
57. _____
58. _____
59. _____
60. _____
61. _____
62. _____
63. _____
64. _____
65. _____
66. _____
67. _____
68. _____
69. _____
70. _____
71. _____

Groom's:

53. _____
54. _____
55. _____
56. _____
57. _____
58. _____
59. _____
60. _____
61. _____
62. _____
63. _____
64. _____
65. _____
66. _____
67. _____
68. _____
69. _____
70. _____
71. _____

Bride's:

72. _____
73. _____
74. _____
75. _____
76. _____
77. _____
78. _____
79. _____
80. _____
81. _____
82. _____
83. _____
84. _____
85. _____
86. _____
87. _____
88. _____
89. _____
90. _____

Groom's:

72. _____
73. _____
74. _____
75. _____
76. _____
77. _____
78. _____
79. _____
80. _____
81. _____
82. _____
83. _____
84. _____
85. _____
86. _____
87. _____
88. _____
89. _____
90. _____

Bride's:

91. _____
92. _____
93. _____
94. _____
95. _____
96. _____
97. _____
98. _____
99. _____
100. _____

Groom's:

91. _____
92. _____
93. _____
94. _____
95. _____
96. _____
97. _____
98. _____
99. _____
100. _____

INVITATIONS, ANNOUNCEMENTS, THANK-YOU NOTES, AND PROGRAMS

With all of the options that you have in these departments, you will need to keep them straight. Fill out the following information, and if you can get a sample, number the information and sample. That way you know where you got it and where to order them from. Remember to make copies of these pages as you need them.

Six months before the wedding, you can have a "Save the date" card sent out. These cards have a magnet or sticker for your guests to remember to save your special date.

Invitations:

Where:_____
Phone Number:_____
Address:_____
_____
_____
How Many:_____
Cost:_____
Description:_____
What They Say:_____
_____
_____

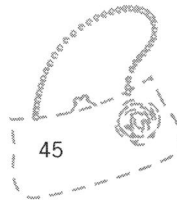

Announcements:

Where:_____

Phone Number:_____

Address:_____

_____

_____

How Many:_____

Cost:_____

Description:_____

What They Say:_____

_____

_____

Thank-you Notes:

Where:_____

Phone Number:_____

Address:_____

_____

_____

How Many:_____

Cost:_____

Description:_____

_____

_____

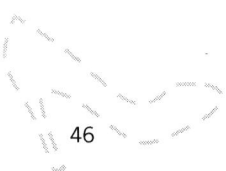

Programs:

Where:_____

Phone Number:_____

Address:_____
_____
_____

How Many:_____

Cost:_____

Introduction:_____
_____
_____
_____

Who Will Be Listed:_____
_____
_____
_____
_____

Directions to Reception:_____
_____
_____
_____
_____

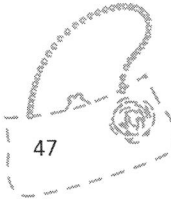

Program Delivery/Pick up:

Who:_____

Where:_____

_____

_____

When:_____

_____

Contact Number:_____

YOUR VOWS

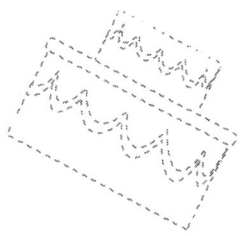

You will remember these words forever because you mean them. They don't have to be anything extravagant, just how you feel. You can have your officiate read the classic version and then add a few words just between the two of you. Or you can write the whole thing yourselves. This is a time when you're proclaiming your true feelings for this wonderful person in front of all of your friends and family, and it should be special. So take the time in this section to write down a few words or the whole service for you and you special someone.

_____

_____

_____

_____

_____

_____

Your Vows... *continued*:

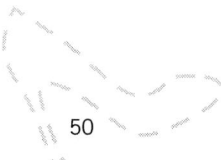

THE DRESSES

This part of the templates is different. This is a part that you fill out, cut out, and fill with pictures of the dresses you try on. You can also use this part for the bridesmaids' dresses. Fill out the information below and put it in the picture pages with the pictures. That way, when you are making a choice, you know where the dress is and all of the information. Not to mention, the picture will remind you exactly what it looked like. Remember when taking the pictures to take front and back pictures.

Name:_____

Phone Number:_____

Address:_____

_____

_____

Dress Size:_____

Style Number:_____

Deposit:_____

Name:_____
Phone Number:_____
Address:_____
_____
_____
Dress Size:_____
Style Number:_____
Deposit:_____

Name:_____
Phone Number:_____
Address:_____
_____
_____
Dress Size:_____
Style Number:_____
Deposit:_____

Name:_____

Phone Number:_____

Address:_____

_____

_____

Dress Size:_____

Style Number:_____

Deposit:_____

Name:_____

Phone Number:_____

Address:_____

_____

_____

Dress Size:_____

Style Number:_____

Deposit:_____

WEDDING PLANNER PROJECT

Name:_____
Phone Number:_____
Address:_____
_____
_____
Dress Size:_____
Style Number:_____
Deposit:_____

Name:_____
Phone Number:_____
Address:_____
_____
_____
Dress Size:_____
Style Number:_____
Deposit:_____

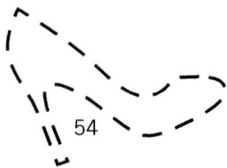

BEAUTY (HAIR AND NAILS)

This section is to help you find a great spa and/or beauty shop to meet your needs for preparation of your wedding day. If you have a large party, they might want you to make a deposit and an appointment in advance. So shop around for the best price and atmosphere for you.

Name:_____

Phone Number:_____

Address:_____

_____

_____

Dates Available:_____

Times Available:_____

Price:_____

Deposit:_____

What is provided for the price:_____

_____

_____

Thoughts/feelings:_____

_____

_____

Name:_____

Phone Number:_____

Address:_____

_____

_____

Dates Available:_____

Times Available:_____

Price:_____

Deposit:_____

What is provided for the price:_____

_____

_____

Thoughts/feelings:_____

_____

_____

Name:_____

THE SUITS

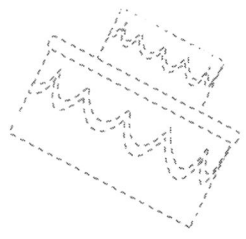

Find the right suit for your man and his boys. But make sure you shop around. You might get a better deal if all the guys go together to get their suits. Some shops give discounts to wedding parties.

Name:_____
Phone Number:_____
Address:_____
_____
_____
Cost to Rent:_____
Cost To Buy:_____

Name:_____
Phone Number:_____
Address:_____
_____
_____
Cost to Rent:_____
Cost To Buy:_____

Name:_____
Phone Number:_____
Address:_____
_____
_____
Cost to Rent:_____
Cost To Buy:_____

Name:_____
Phone Number:_____
Address:_____
_____
_____
Cost to Rent:_____
Cost To Buy:_____

Delivery/Pick Up: _____
Who: _____
When: _____
Where: _____
_____
_____
Contact Number: _____

FLORIST

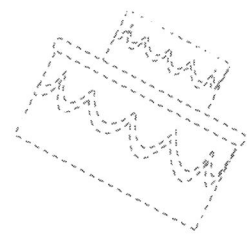

The florist is another very important part of your wedding. They help set the stage with elegance and color. The right florist could be very hard to find or right next door. However, you need to find one that you feel is right for you. Shop around.

Name:_____

Phone Number:_____

Address:_____

_____

_____

Price:_____

What is provided for the price:_____

_____

_____

Thoughts/feelings:_____

_____

_____

Name:_____

Phone Number:_____

Address:_____

_____

_____

Price:_____

What is provided for the price:_____

_____

_____

Thoughts/feelings:_____

_____

_____

Name:_____

Phone Number:_____

Address:_____

_____

_____

Price:_____

What is provided for the price:_____

_____

_____

Thoughts/feelings:_____

_____

_____

FLOWERS

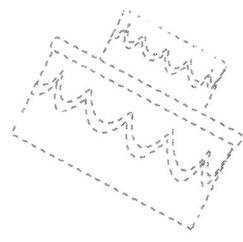

Take this section with you when you are talking to different florists. This way you remember everything that you want and can write down ideas you might get along the way. This is just for you to remember what you want down to a T.

Bridal Bouquet Description:_____
_____
_____
_____

Bridal Toss Bouquet Description: _____
_____
_____
_____

Flower Girl Flowers Description: _____
_____
_____
_____

Maid of Honor Bouquet Description: _____
_____
_____
_____

Corsages Description and Number: _____
_____
_____
_____

Boutonnieres Description and Number: _____
_____
_____
_____

Ceremony Flowers and Description: _____
_____
_____
_____

Reception Flowers and Description: _____
_____
_____
_____

Delivery/Pick Up: _____
Who: _____
When: _____
Where: _____
_____
_____
Contact Number: _____

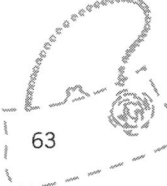

CATERERS

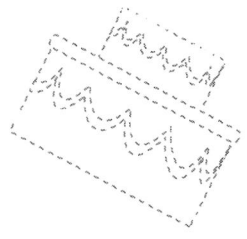

This is the only way to remember who you talked to about who will be serving your food. Some venues that you rent will have their own catering, and that makes it easy. But if they don't, shop around.

Ask the caterers to have food for you while you are getting ready. Also, ask if they can prepare to-go boxes for you and the groom for when you leave the reception in case you didn't to eat at the reception.

Name:_____

Phone Number:_____

Address:_____

_____

_____

Price:_____

What is provided for the price:_____

_____

_____

Thoughts/feelings:_____

_____

_____

Name:_____

Phone Number:_____

Address:_____

_____

_____

Price:_____

What is provided for the price:_____

_____

_____

Thoughts/feelings:_____

_____

_____

        Delivery/Pick Up: _____

        Who: _____

        When: _____

        Where: _____

        _____

        _____

        Contact Number: _____

THE FOOD

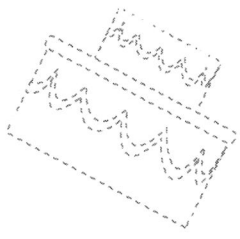

This is one part, besides the dress, that everyone is going to remember. Make sure it is what you want, and remember to taste everything! You might be surprised how hungry you are after the ceremony, so make sure that you and all the other hungry people get enough. (And that there is some leftover to take home!)

Buffet or Service Description: _____
_____
_____
_____
_____

Meats: _____
_____
_____
_____

Fruits and Veggies: _____
_____
_____
_____

Pastas: _____
_____
_____

Salads: _____
_____
_____

Finger Foods: _____
_____
_____
_____

Desserts: _____
_____
_____
_____

Drinks: _____
_____
_____

Open Bar: _____
_____
_____

Wine List: _____
_____
_____
_____

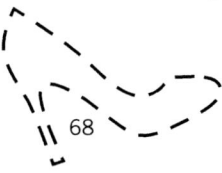

THE CAKE

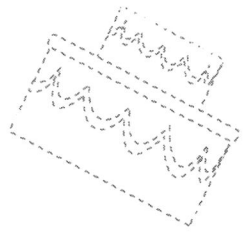

The cake is a big part of your reception. You want the cake to be original, classic, or just plain beautiful, so you should shop around for the best price, taste, and design. This section will help you keep it all straight. Remember, taste!

Name:_____

Phone Number:_____

Address:_____

_____

_____

Price:_____

What is provided for the price:_____

_____

_____

Thoughts/feelings:_____

_____

_____

Name:_____

Phone Number:_____

Address:_____

_____

_____

Price:_____

What is provided for the price:_____

_____

_____

Thoughts/feelings:_____

_____

_____

Delivery/Pick Up: _____

Who: _____

When: _____

Where: _____

_____

_____

Contact Number: _____

RECEPTION

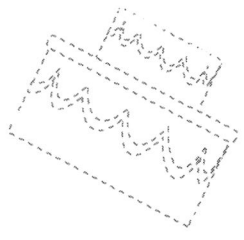

This is a party to end all parties. Or it is your Cinderella ball. Either way, make it memorable, make it fun, and make it about you and your new hubby. This section, like many others, gives you the chance to look around and find what you want all while remembering where everything is.

Name:_____

Phone Number:_____

Address:_____

_____

_____

Dates Available:_____

Times Available:_____

Price:_____

What is provided for the price:_____

_____

_____

Thoughts/feelings:_____

_____

_____

Name:_____
Phone Number:_____
Address:_____
_____

Dates Available:_____
Times Available:_____
Price:_____
What is provided for the price:_____
_____
_____
_____

Thoughts/feelings:_____
_____
_____
_____

Name:_____

Phone Number:_____

Address:_____

_____

_____

Dates Available:_____

Times Available:_____

Price:_____

What is provided for the price:_____

_____

_____

_____

_____

Thoughts/feelings:_____

_____

_____

_____

_____

RECEPTION DÉCOR

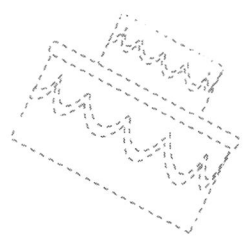

This is a section for you to write out what you want every aspect of your reception to look like—everything from the guestbook to the silverware. Leave no detail out. This is a reflection of your ceremony and of you; make it perfectly you.

Entrance Description:_____
_____
_____

Gift Table Description:_____
_____
_____

Guest Book Table:_____
_____
_____

Bar:_____
_____
_____

Guest Tables:_____
_____
_____

Music Stage: _____
_____
_____

Buffet: _____
_____
_____

Lighting: _____
_____
_____

Cake Table: _____
_____
_____

Wedding Party Table: _____
_____
_____

Wall Décor: _____
_____
_____

SEATING ARRANGEMENTS

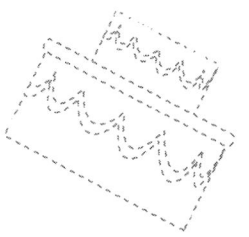

This is the party where you get to decide who sits with whom. If you are having a formal reception, you have to pick the seating arrangement.

Table 1

1. _____
2. _____
3. _____
4. _____
5. _____
6. _____
7. _____
8. _____

Table 2

1. _____
2. _____
3. _____
4. _____
5. _____
6. _____
7. _____
8. _____

Table 3

1. _____
2. _____
3. _____
4. _____
5. _____
6. _____
7. _____
8. _____

Table 4

1. _____
2. _____
3. _____
4. _____
5. _____
6. _____
7. _____
8. _____

Table 5

1. _____
2. _____
3. _____
4. _____
5. _____
6. _____
7. _____
8. _____

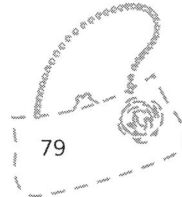

Table 6

1. _____
2. _____
3. _____
4. _____
5. _____
6. _____
7. _____
8. _____

Table 7

1. _____
2. _____
3. _____
4. _____
5. _____
6. _____
7. _____
8. _____

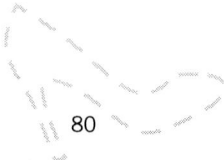

Table 8

1. _____
2. _____
3. _____
4. _____
5. _____
6. _____
7. _____
8. _____

Table 9

1. _____
2. _____
3. _____
4. _____
5. _____
6. _____
7. _____
8. _____

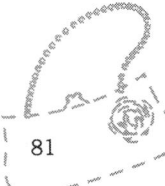

Table 10

1. _____
2. _____
3. _____
4. _____
5. _____
6. _____
7. _____
8. _____

Table 11

1. _____
2. _____
3. _____
4. _____
5. _____
6. _____
7. _____
8. _____

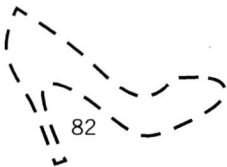

FAVORS

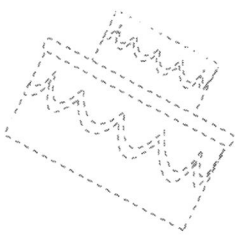

The wedding favors are the wonderful little matchbooks with you and your soon-to-be's name and wedding date on them. They are the cute little plastic champagne glasses with candy in them. They are whatever you want them to be that your guests can take home with them to remember the event. When shopping for wedding favors, you are going to want to look online, in catalogs, and in stores. This section will help you keep it all straight.

Name:_____

Phone Number:_____

Address:_____

_____

_____

Count:_____

Price:_____

Description:_____

_____

Thoughts/feelings:_____

_____

_____

WEDDING PLANNER PROJECT

Name:_____
Phone Number:_____
Address:_____
_____
_____

Count:_____
Price:_____
Description:_____
_____

Thoughts/feelings:_____
_____
_____

Name:_____
Phone Number:_____
Address:_____
_____
_____

Count:_____
Price:_____
Description:_____
_____

Thoughts/feelings:_____
_____
_____

PICTURES/VIDEO

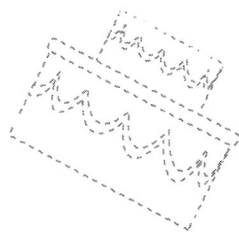

This section is to help you compare prices for photographers and videographers. Really shop around for these. Talk to your friends and look at the portfolios of the photographers. After the honeymoon is no time to wonder if you made the right choice.

Name:_____

Phone Number:_____

Address:_____

_____

_____

Dates Available:_____

Times Available:_____

Price:_____

Deposit:_____

What is provided for the price:_____

_____

_____

Thoughts/feelings:_____

_____

_____

Name:_____
Phone Number:_____
Address:_____
_____
_____

Dates Available:_____
Times Available:_____
Price:_____
Deposit:_____
What is provided for the price:_____
_____
_____

Thoughts/feelings:_____
_____
_____

MUSIC

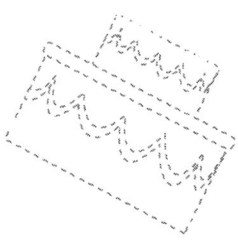

This section is for you to write down the information about the musical entertainment that you are thinking about having at your wedding. This way, when the time comes for you to make a final decision, you have all of the information in front of you and can make an informed decision.

Name:_____

Phone Number:_____

Address:_____

_____

_____

Dates Available:_____

Times Available:_____

Price:_____

Deposit:_____

What is provided for the price:_____

_____

_____

Thoughts/feelings:_____

_____

_____

Name:_____

Phone Number:_____

Address:_____

_____

_____

Dates Available:_____

Times Available:_____

Price:_____

Deposit:_____

What is provided for the price:_____

_____

_____

Thoughts/feelings:_____

_____

_____

THE DANCES

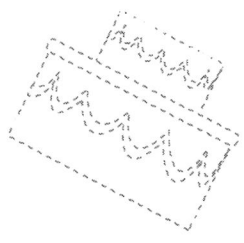

The dances are important. You will always remember the song that you and your new hubby danced to. Make it special and meaningful. Take this with you when you hire someone to do the music so that you remember who is dancing to what.

Bride and Groom Dance:_____
_____
_____

Father of the Bride and Bride:_____
_____
_____

Other dances:_____
_____
_____
_____
_____
_____

GIFT LIST

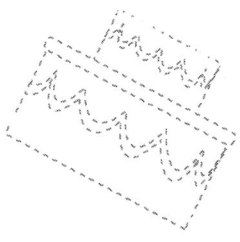

In this section, write the name of the person each gift came from and what the gift is. That way when you write your thank-you notes, you can keep it all straight and make the thank-you notes more personal.

From:_____
Gift: _____

From:_____
Gift: _____

From:_____
Gift: _____

From:_____
Gift: _____

From:_____
Gift: _____

From:_____
Gift: _____

From:_____
Gift: _____

From:_____
Gift: _____

From:_____
Gift: _____

From:_____
Gift: _____

From:_____
Gift: _____

From:_____
Gift: _____

From:_____
Gift: _____

From:_____
Gift: _____

From:_____
Gift: _____

From:_____
Gift: _____

From:_____
Gift: _____

From:_____
Gift: _____

From:_____
Gift: _____

From:_____
Gift: _____

From:_____
Gift: _____

From:_____
Gift: _____

From:_____
Gift: _____

From:_____
Gift: _____

From:_____
Gift: _____

From:_____
Gift: _____

From:_____
Gift: _____

From:_____
Gift: _____

From:_____
Gift: _____

From:_____
Gift: _____

From:_____
Gift: _____

From:_____
Gift: _____

TRANSPORTATION

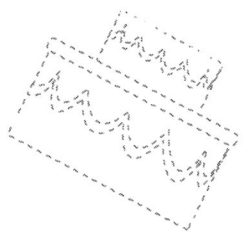

Call around and get all of the information before you decide. I have said that over and over again through out this book. Why? Because it is important to know what you are getting for your money. You should do this with all of the wedding planning. You also have to keep it all straight. Calling around to different companies for transportation, that information goes here.

Name:_____
Phone Number:_____
Address:_____
_____
_____
Dates Available:_____
Times Available:_____
Price:_____
Deposit:_____
What is provided for the price:_____
_____
_____
Thoughts/feelings:_____
_____
_____

Name:_____
Phone Number:_____
Address:_____
_____
_____

Dates Available:_____
Times Available:_____
Price:_____
Deposit:_____
What is provided for the price:_____
_____
_____

Thoughts/feelings:_____
_____
_____

THE HONEYMOON

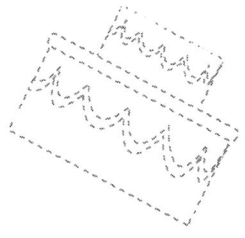

This will make choosing the right honeymoon destination a breeze. Sit down with your honey and pick the places that you would most like to go. Write them in the available spaces and weigh your options.

Option One:

Where: _____
Travel Plans: _____
_____
_____
_____
Staying: _____
Cost: _____

Option Two:

Where: _____
Travel Plans: _____
_____
_____
Staying: _____
Cost: _____

Option Three:

Where:_____
Travel Plans: _____
_____
_____
Staying: _____
Cost: _____

Option Four:

Where:_____
Travel Plans: _____
_____
_____
Staying: _____
Cost: _____

Option Five:

Where:_____
Travel Plans: _____
_____
_____
Staying: _____
Cost: _____

THE REHEARSAL DINNER

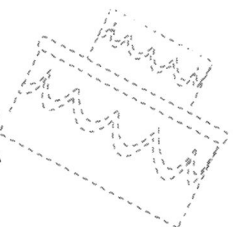

This section is one that I think is overlooked from time to time. Write out where the dinner will be, and then make a copy of this page and give it to the wedding party. That way you know that everybody knows. Then keep your copy and write down who you gave it to. That way nobody gets left out.

The rehearsal dinner will take place at:_____

_____

Directions: _____

_____

_____

_____

_____

Time: _____

Who the reminder was given too:_____

_____

_____

_____

_____

WEDDING PLANNER PROJECT

THE WAY IT GOES

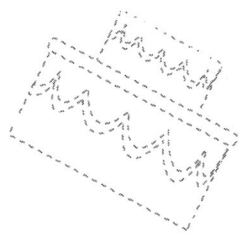

This is a time table to let everyone at the rehearsal know what is going on. This should be copied and given to the photographer, the videographer, the entertainment, the catering staff, the cake delivery person, the florist, and the entire wedding party. This is ultimately the way you want things timed to happen.

Photographer arrival:_____

Florist arrival:_____

Cake arrival:_____

Catering arrival:_____

Music arrival:_____

Ushers arrival:_____

Processional Order/Time:_____

Ceremony Time:_____

Ceremony Length:_____

Recessional Order/Time:_____

Photo Session Time:_____

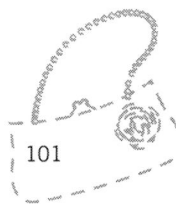

DELEGATE

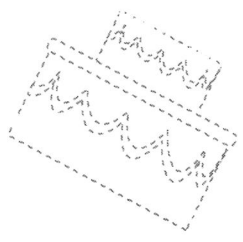

Y‍ou are not going to want to, have time to, or should have to do everything. So delegate. Just remember who is doing what and how you can get a hold of them at a moment's notice.

Who:_____

What:_____

_____

_____

_____

Name:_____

_____

Phone Number:_____

Who:_____

What:_____

_____

_____

_____

Name:_____

_____

Phone Number:_____

Who:_____
What:_____
_____
_____
_____
Name:_____
_____
Phone Number:_____

Who:_____
What:_____
_____
_____
_____
Name:_____
_____
Phone Number:_____

Who:_____
What:_____
_____
_____
_____
Name:_____
_____
Phone Number:_____

Who:_____

What:_____

_____

_____

_____

Name:_____

_____

Phone Number:_____

Who:_____

What:_____

_____

_____

_____

Name:_____

_____

Phone Number:_____

Who:_____

What:_____

_____

_____

_____

Name:_____

_____

Phone Number:_____

FINISHING TOUCHES

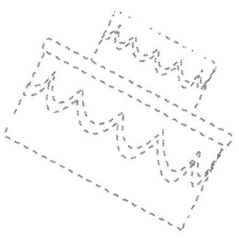

These are all the little additions that not everybody thinks about until the last minute. Again, use what you want and leave the rest.

Bride's Finishing Touches:

Veil or Headpiece:

Style Number:_____
Cost: _____
Where: _____
Phone Number: _____
Address: _____
_____
_____

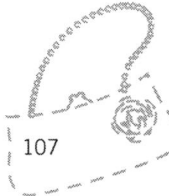

Shoes:

Style Number:_____
Cost: _____
Where: _____
Phone Number: _____
Address: _____
_____
_____

Hosiery:

Style Number:_____
Cost: _____
Where: _____
Phone Number: _____
Address: _____
_____
_____

Slip:

Style Number:_____
Cost: _____
Where: _____
Phone Number: _____
Address: _____
_____
_____

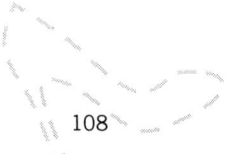

Bra:

Style Number:_____

Cost: _____

Where: _____

Phone Number: _____

Address: _____

_____

_____

Gloves:

Style Number:_____

Cost: _____

Where: _____

Phone Number: _____

Address: _____

_____

_____

Jewelry:

Style Number:_____

Cost: _____

Where: _____

Phone Number: _____

Address: _____

_____

_____

Garter:

Style Number:_____
Cost: _____
Where: _____
Phone Number: _____
Address: _____
_____
_____

Shoes:

Style Number:_____
Cost: _____
Where: _____
Phone Number: _____
Address: _____
_____
_____

Socks:

Style Number:_____
Cost: _____
Where: _____
Phone Number: _____
Address: _____
_____
_____

Hat:

Style Number:_____

Cost: _____

Where: _____

Phone Number: _____

Address: _____

_____

_____

Gloves:

Style Number:_____

Cost: _____

Where: _____

_____

Phone Number: _____

Address: _____

_____

_____

CONCLUSION

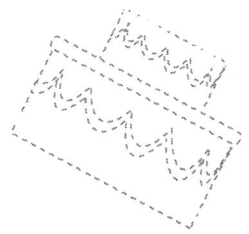

That's it! You have done it! Down to every perfect detail. You have made the book work perfectly for you, and now your wedding will do the same. Now that you are so organized, your day will be flawless.

I hope that you have found the pages of this book as helpful as I did. Thank you for letting me help make your day perfect.

I hope that you and your soon-to-be husband have a happy and healthy life together. I wish you two all the best!

Notes

Notes

Notes

Notes

Notes

Notes